RUN FOR YOUR LIFE!

Predators and Prey on the African Savanna

by LOLA M. SCHAEFER

illustrated by
PAUL MEISEL

Holiday House / New York

For Mason
—L. M. S.

For my parents
—P. M.

The publisher would like to thank Melinda Weaver, PhD candidate
at Arizona State University, for her expert review of this book.

Printed and Bound in November 2015
at Toppan Leefung, DongGuan City, China.
The artwork was created with watercolor and acrylic
on Strathmore paper, with digital enhancement.
www.holidayhouse.com
First Edition
1 3 5 7 9 10 8 6 4 2

Library of Congress Cataloging-in-Publication Data
Schaefer, Lola M., 1950- author.
Run for your life! : predators and prey on the African savanna / by Lola M. Schaefer;
illustrated by Paul Meisel. — First edition.
pages cm
Audience: Ages 4–8.
Audience: K to grade 3.
ISBN 978-0-8234-3555-5 (hardcover)
1. Savanna animals—Juvenile literature.
2. Animal locomotion—Juvenile literature.
3. Speed—Juvenile literature. I. Meisel, Paul, illustrator.
II. Title.
QL115.3.S33 2016
591.7'48—dc23
2015017498

Every day on the African
savanna, animals search
for food. Some eat only meat,
which makes them
predators. They chase
their prey across the plains,
sometimes catching their
next meal, sometimes not.
It's a real-life game
of hide-and-seek.

On the savanna,
animals sleep.

Then . . .
leopards spring,
and impalas bound.

Eagles swoop,
and hares hop.

*Crocodiles lunge,
and hippos trot.*

Cheetahs leap,
and ostriches scurry.

*Jackals pounce,
and giraffes lope.*

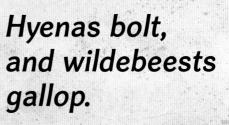

Hyenas bolt,
and wildebeests
gallop.

*Wild dogs rush,
and zebras stampede.*

Snakes slither,
and elephants
lumber.

Caracals jump,
and monkeys scramble.

Across the savanna,
they scamper and skitter,
past termites
and aardvarks,
near watering holes
and rhinos.

They plunge and pitch
across streams
and trails,
over rocks
and hills.

They stomp and tramp
under trees
and vultures,
around bushes
and buffalo.

They chase and gain,
sprint and flee,
until . . .

lions stand.

RUN...for your life!

On the savanna,
animals sleep.

Many animals that live on the savanna stay alive through camouflage and speed. Both coloring and markings help some creatures blend into their surroundings. But predators such as leopards, hyenas, caracals, jackals, wild dogs, cheetahs and lions rely on their cunning and speed to surprise and capture prey. There are many chase-and-flee scenes between predators and prey played out on the savanna every day.

The patas monkey and the black mamba snake, both shown in this book, are two of the fastest animals in their families. The patas monkey spends most of its day down on the ground. It can jet from 0 mph to 35 mph (56 km/h) in three seconds. The black mamba can slither up to 12.5 mph (20 km/h), which is an amazing feat for a snake. Here are the average sprint speeds for the animals mentioned in this book.

black mamba snake	12.5 mph	(20 km/h)
crocodile (swim)	22 mph	(35 km/h)
African bush elephant	25 mph	(40 km/h)
hippopotamus	30 mph	(48 km/h)
giraffe	32 mph	(52 km/h)
aardvark	35 mph	(56 km/h)
buffalo	35 mph	(56 km/h)
leopard	35 mph	(56 km/h)
patas monkey	35 mph	(56 km/h)

rhinoceros	35 mph	(56 km/h)
hyena	40 mph	(64 km/h)
jackal	40 mph	(64 km/h)
ostrich	40 mph	(64 km/h)
zebra	40 mph	(64 km/h)
African hare	45 mph	(72 km/h)
wild dog	45 mph	(72 km/h)
caracal	50 mph	(80 km/h)
lion	50 mph	(80 km/h)
wildebeest	50 mph	(80 km/h)
impala	55 mph	(89 km/h)
martial eagle (fly)	60 mph	(97 km/h)
vulture (fly)	60 mph	(97 km/h)
cheetah	70 mph	(113 km/h)
martial eagle (dive)	100 mph	(161 km/h)